Water, Wind and Solar Power

Editor: John Clark
Editorial Planning: Clark Robinson Ltd
Design: David West
                     Children's Book Design
Illustrator: Peter Harper
Picture research: Cecilia Weston-Baker
Photographic Credits:
Cover and pages 4-5, 9, 10-11, 17, 18-19, 21, 23, 24, 25, 26-27, 28 right and 29
bottom: J. Allan Cash Library; page 6: British Nuclear Fuels Ltd; pages 8, 12,
14-15 and 16: Robert Harding Library; page 13: Mary Evans Picture Library;
page 12-13: Bruce Coleman Ltd; page 20: Science Photo Library; page 22:
Spectrum Colour Library; page 26: Sandia Laboratories; pages 28 left and 29
top: Topham Picture Library.

First published in
the United States in 1990 by
Franklin Watts
387 Park Avenue South
New York NY 10016

The publishers would like to acknowledge that the photographs reproduced
within this book have been posed by models or have been obrained from
photographic agencies.

For information regarding permission, write to
Franklin Watts
387 Park Avenue South
New York, NY 10016

This edition is reprinted by arrangement with
Franklin Watts
Macmillan/McGraw-Hill School Division
10 Union Square East
New York, New York 10003

Printed and bound in Mexico.
ISBN 0-02-274939-X

1 2 3 4 5 6 7 8 9 REY 99 98 97 96 95 94 93 92

Facts on

Water, Wind and Solar Power

Guy Arnold

Macmillan/McGraw-Hill School Publishing Company
New York Chicago Columbus

4

CONTENTS

RENEWABLE ENERGY
6

WIND POWER
8

WIND ON WATER
12

WATER POWER
14

TIDAL POWER
22

SOLAR POWER
24

WORLD CLIMATES
30

GLOSSARY
31

INDEX
32

INTRODUCTION

At present, most of the world's energy comes from coal, gas, or oil – the fossil fuels – or from nuclear power. The first three of these power sources are being used up at an ever-growing rate. Oil supplies, for example, are expected to run out in about 50 years' time. Nuclear power poses special problems and dangers, and many people fear the possibility of terrible nuclear accidents. The world is now seeking to develop alternative sources of energy to replace the fossil fuels as they are used up. The rapid growth of the world's population, and the modernization of developing countries, puts further pressure on existing energy resources. There is a growing worldwide search for new sources of energy to meet all our needs. In fact, there are huge resources available in the form of heat from the Sun (solar energy), from the wind, and from water power. The difficulty lies in harnessing this energy: how do we turn the Sun's heat or the ocean's waves into electricity? The advantage of solar, wind and water energy is that they can never be exhausted. As long as our planet exists, these sources of power will continue to be available, which is why we call their energy renewable.

◁ Old water wheel, Sussex, England.

RENEWABLE ENERGY

Energy is obtained from two kinds of sources. The first kind includes the fuels that are in common use – coal, natural gas and oil – but once these have been burned to provide energy they are gone forever. Elements such as uranium are sources of nuclear power, and because they can be reprocessed, they are effectively inexhaustible. But nuclear power presents very special problems of its own. The second kind includes heat from the Sun, wind power, and water power. This energy can be tapped forever, which is why it is called renewable. Whichever source of power is being used – such as coal or water flow – we have to make devices to turn the power into usable energy. A thermal power station converts coal into electricity; a water wheel allows water to drive a machine.

NO RETURN

Renewable energy will continue as long as this planet remains habitable. Unlike fossil fuels, renewable energy is clean and does not create dangerous waste materials (except for nuclear power, which is made from an element called uranium and does create radioactive waste). These spent fuel rods (below), used to produce nuclear power, are now useless, but they must be carefully stored because they remain radioactive and dangerous. The huge stockpiles of coal represent the most abundant of our fossil fuels, but coal, too, will run out eventually.

POLLUTION

In recent years most people have begun to worry more about pollution. Huge power stations like this one pour waste out into the air, which in turn leads to acid rain. There are many other forms of pollution, such as oil slicks in the sea, and the discharge of waste matter from factories into rivers.

REPLACING FOSSIL FUELS

The diagram shows what may happen over the next 100 years. The three disks — the largest at the bottom for 1990, the smallest at the top for 2090 — are divided into segments to represent energy sources. Today almost all of our energy comes from oil, coal, gas and nuclear power. However, over the next century the segments representing today's main sources of energy get smaller or disappear. But the segments representing renewable energy will become larger.

1990   50yrs

100yrs

Key

Non Renewable

Coal	Nuclear
Oil	Gas

Renewable

Wind	Biomass
Hydro	Solar

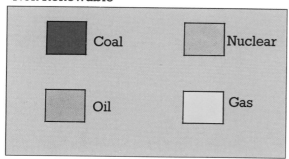

8 WIND POWER

The wind can be terrifying, and the destructive force of a hurricane can flatten a town. But wind energy has been harnessed by man since ancient times. It is used in two main ways: to drive windmills on land, and to drive sailing vessels at sea. Traditionally, windmills were used to grind corn or to pump water for drainage or irrigation. Modern windmills generate electricity. The use of wind power is not highly developed, and there are many difficulties to overcome. There is also the problem that the wind does not always blow. Yet once the problems have been solved, the amount of wind energy available is enormous. Britain, for example, has enough wind blowing along its western coasts to produce one third of its electricity needs.

IRRIGATION

Irrigation is one of the oldest farming techniques in the world. It involves moving water (from a lake or river) and spreading it evenly over an area of land to be cultivated. Windmills have long been used for this purpose, and although they are not particularly efficient, they provide a cheap way of moving water. Many traditional windmills are still used for this purpose today.

EARLY WINDMILLS

A common traditional type of windmill has a conical or pyramid-shaped tower, and works by the action of wind against its sails or vanes. These are attached to a windshaft, which is a horizontal axle that holds the sails vertical to catch the maximum wind. The windshaft is connected by gears inside the mill to a vertical shaft. This rotates and drives a pump or other machinery at the base of the windmill tower. The machinery of traditional mills is heavy and complex, with a series of interlocking cogwheels. Although often made of wood, they usually last for many years without needing repairs.

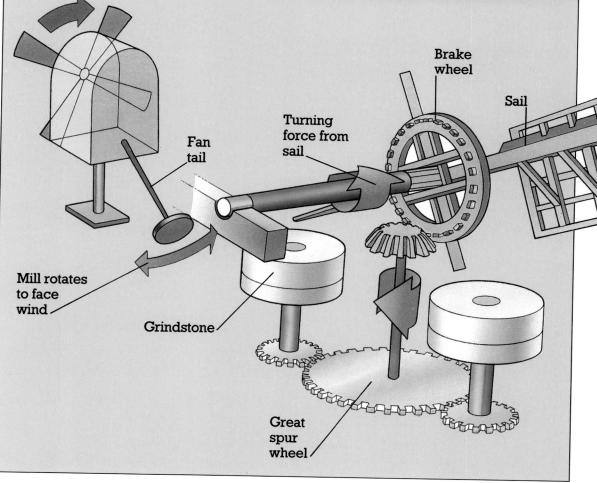

Brake wheel

Sail

Turning force from sail

Fan tail

Mill rotates to face wind

Grindstone

Great spur wheel

WIND POWER

MILLS FOR ELECTRICITY

So far, attempts to use windmills to generate electricity on a large scale have failed. Most modern windmills are small, designed to charge batteries or provide electricity for isolated farms. Propeller-type windmills are best for harnessing wind power. But to harness wind on a large scale would require giant windmills. It has been estimated that to produce the equivalent output of an ordinary coal-fired power station would require 50 windmills the height of the Eiffel Tower.

▽ Windmills in use on the plateau of Lasithi, Crete.

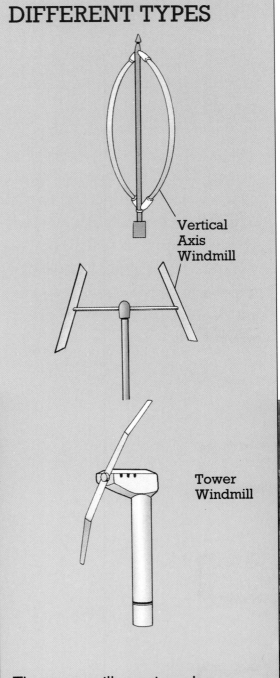

DIFFERENT TYPES

Vertical Axis Windmill

Tower Windmill

The top two illustrations show vertical axis windmills. The blades move around horizontally. These react to wind from any direction without having to turn to face the wind. The bottom tower windmill is a more traditional design.

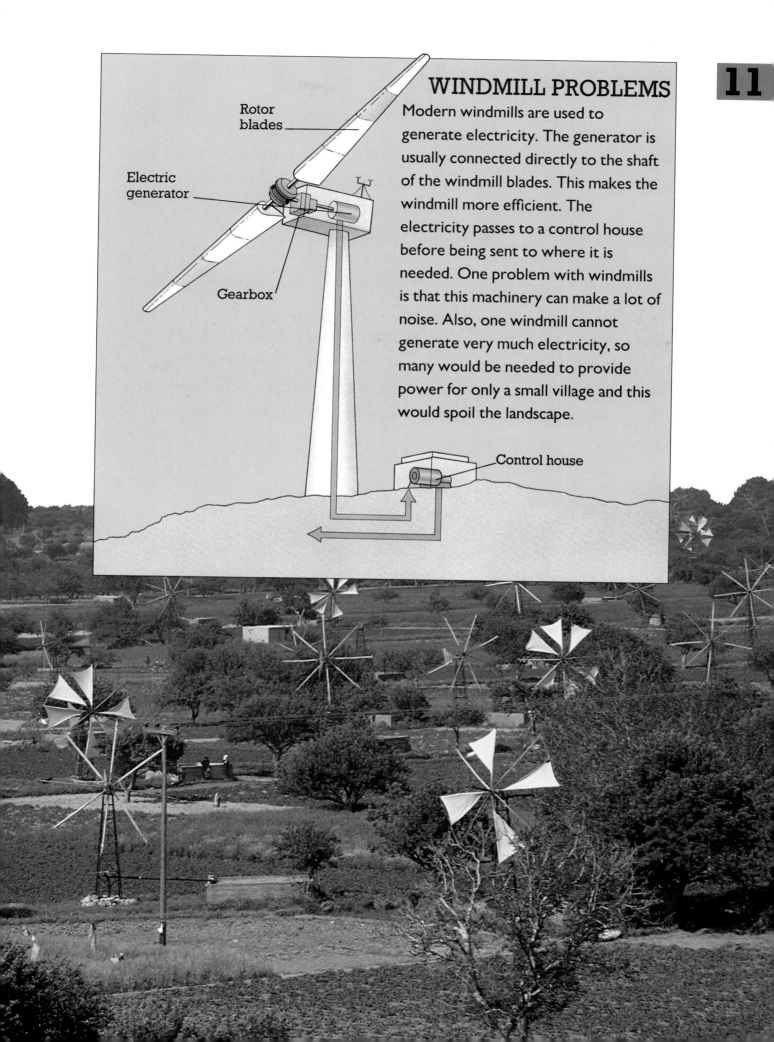

WINDMILL PROBLEMS

Rotor blades

Electric generator

Gearbox

Modern windmills are used to generate electricity. The generator is usually connected directly to the shaft of the windmill blades. This makes the windmill more efficient. The electricity passes to a control house before being sent to where it is needed. One problem with windmills is that this machinery can make a lot of noise. Also, one windmill cannot generate very much electricity, so many would be needed to provide power for only a small village and this would spoil the landscape.

Control house

WIND ON WATER

The use of wind power to propel ships through the water has a very long history. The ancient Egyptians, Greeks, Phoenicians, and Romans all used sailing vessels. Slowly through the ages, sail power was developed and refined, from the single square sail used in the ancient world, to nineteenth-century merchantmen which carried as many as 25 separate sails. The coming of steam power in the mid-nineteenth century meant an end to the great days of sailing. There are exceptions, and today, although most of the world's shipping no longer uses sails for power, Arab dhows still carry merchandise across the Indian Ocean between the Gulf and East Africa. Also, yachts and sailing dinghies provide entertainment and relaxation for many people.

▽ Junk in Hong Kong harbor

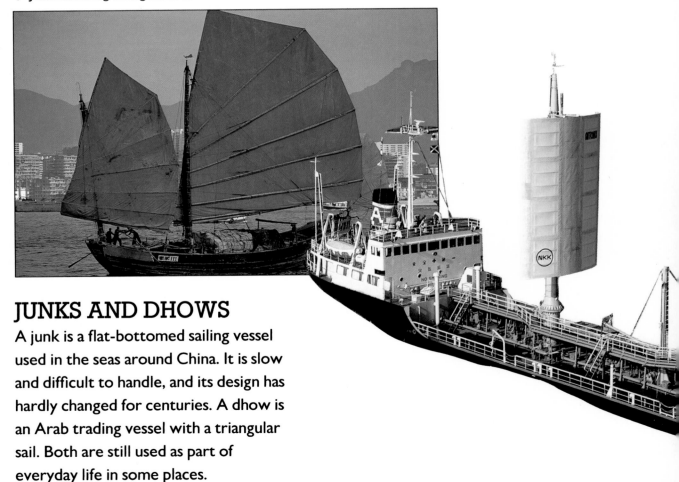

JUNKS AND DHOWS

A junk is a flat-bottomed sailing vessel used in the seas around China. It is slow and difficult to handle, and its design has hardly changed for centuries. A dhow is an Arab trading vessel with a triangular sail. Both are still used as part of everyday life in some places.

TEA CLIPPER

The tea clippers of the nineteenth century were made very long and narrow for fast sailing. They were used to carry tea to Great Britain from India and Ceylon. The first clipper to get home each year got the highest price for its tea, so they raced all the way.

MODERN SAILING

The faster we use up fossil fuels, the more important it is to reexamine old ways of doing things. Sail power has been an effective means of transport for thousands of years, and should not be ignored for the future. This Japanese tanker has computer-operated aluminum sails, which save 10 percent of its engine's fuel consumption. A computer linked to the engine and the sails sets the best course according to the wind direction. Experiments have been tried with land yachts propelled by sails. There may be a future for these in travel across deserts or open country.

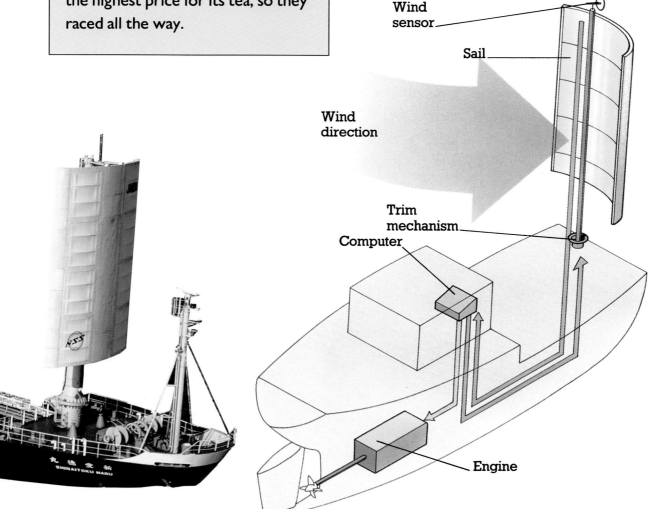

Wind sensor

Sail

Wind direction

Trim mechanism

Computer

Engine

WATER POWER

The force of water is immense and can be very destructive. The waves raised by a storm at sea or on a lake can sink a ship. Alternatively, the force of water can be harnessed as a source of energy. Power comes from the strength of the flow of water. On land, this means using the flow of a river, the fall of a waterfall or an artificially created fall made by building a dam. Traditionally, water power was harnessed by making flowing water turn a water wheel, which drove machinery. Today, most water power is used to drive turbines and generate electricity. If fully harnessed, the power of the Zaire river in Africa could supply 13 percent of the world's total hydroelectric capacity.

OX POWER

Water is one of life's essentials, and putting it to good use has been one of man's earliest occupations. In many parts of the world, oxen are still used as a source of power. In the picture, ox power is being used to move water for irrigating the land.

WATER WHEELS

Water wheels are among the oldest of mechanical inventions and have long been used to drive machinery, especially in mills for grinding corn. There are four main types of water wheel: the overshot wheel, the undershot wheel, the breast wheel and the turbine (see page 16). Overshot and undershot wheels, so-called depending on whether the water flows over or under the wheel, are illustrated here. If a water wheel is given power, it can be used to move water. A large wheel with a series of buckets attached can raise water from a river to irrigate adjoining fields.

Overshot

Undershot

WATER POWER

TURBINES

A turbine revolves from the force of a stream of water, or steam or hot gas, which strikes against its blades to turn a shaft. The basic structure of a water turbine is the shaft, to which can be attached buckets, propeller blades or a number of wheels. The wheels have vanes or blades, and look like a many-bladed fan. The two main types are called impulse turbines and reaction turbines. The shaft of an impulse turbine is turned by the force of water striking the blades. The shaft or rotor of a reaction turbine is turned when the water is deflected by the blades. In a Pelton wheel turbine a jet of water is made to turn through 180° after it hits the bucket-shaped blades. But whatever the technique used the principle is the same: to use the flow of water to turn the turbine to produce energy.

▽ **Turbines in a power station**

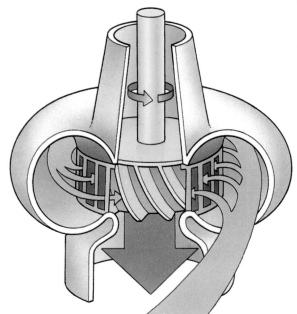

Francis reaction turbine

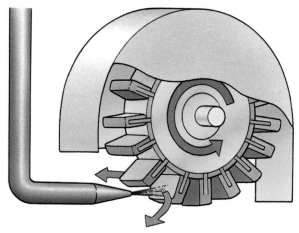

Pelton impulse wheel turbine

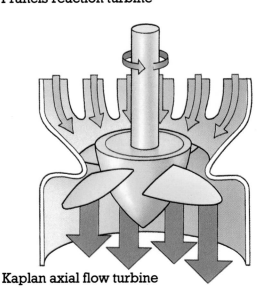

Kaplan axial flow turbine

MAKING ELECTRICITY

Water-driven turbines are mainly used to generate electricity, known as hydroelectricity. The shaft of the turbine is connected directly to the shaft of an electrical generator called an alternator. This has a central spinning magnet surrounded by a coil of wires, so that the coil is always in a moving magnetic field. The result is to create an electric current in the coil. At a hydroelectric power station several very large turbines are used, and these can generate great amounts of electricity. But a small turbine can be used to provide electricity for just one house.

△ Hydroelectric power station

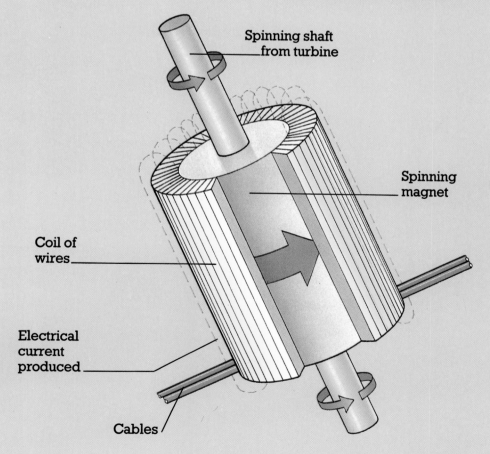

Spinning shaft from turbine

Spinning magnet

Coil of wires

Electrical current produced

Cables

WATER POWER

DAMS

Dams are among the world's greatest engineering achievements. Dam building worldwide, with the exception of China, is at the rate of about 200 dams a year. China is at present building about 1,000 dams a year. About four-fifths of all dams are less than 100ft high. Large dams can cause major environmental problems because the lakes they create flood huge areas. People have to be moved, animal life is disturbed and farming patterns are altered so that the ecology of large areas is unbalanced. The lakes farmed may also eventually silt up. There are several masonry or concrete dams of various shapes, rock-filled dams, and earth dams.

Main Types of Dam

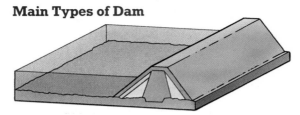

Embankment dam

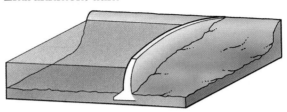

Double curvature dam

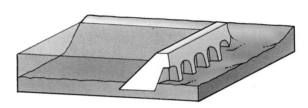

Buttressed straight dam

Arch dam

Arch dam at lake Brauvra

HOW DAMS WORK

The principle of a dam is simple. Wherever possible the dam is sited at the mouth of a gorge or valley so as to force the waters of a river to pile up behind the dam to form a lake. In a typical embankment dam (below) a tunnel carries the water from behind the dam to turbines in the power house. The flow of water into the tunnel is controlled by sluice gates. The greater the drop between the water level behind the dam and the turbines, the greater the force of water and the quantity of electricity generated. From the power house at the foot of the dam, pylons and cables carry the electricity to where it is needed.

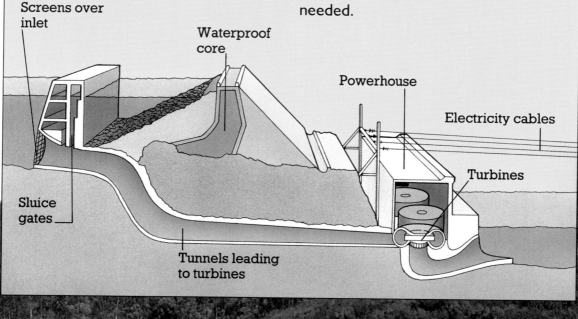

Screens over inlet · Waterproof core · Powerhouse · Electricity cables · Turbines · Sluice gates · Tunnels leading to turbines

WATER POWER

PUMPED STORAGE

Dams are sometimes built in pairs to create two reservoirs. At a time of peak demand for electricity, water is allowed to flow down from the higher to the lower reservoir thus generating electricity. At a time of low demand, spare electricity can be used to pump water from the lower reservoir back up to the higher one, where it can be stored for later use. Such an operation not only stores power, but also saves water. The illustration shows a typical dam construction with two reservoirs, and the system of pipes through which water can move in either direction.

Dam

Upper reservoir

Metal lined
concrete
tunnel

Water flows down
for peak
demand

THE LANDSCAPE

Dams alter the landscape permanently by creating huge lakes. A giant hydroelectric dam may be a structure of awe-inspiring beauty, but it also requires unsightly pylons carrying cables across the countryside. New roads have to be constructed to serve the dam, and new housing must be built for people who have been displaced. Care is needed to protect and preserve the environment.

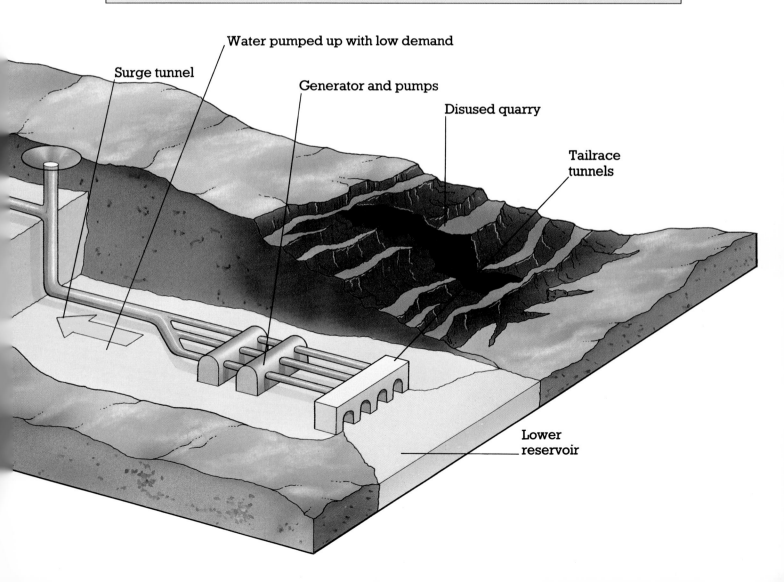

Surge tunnel

Water pumped up with low demand

Generator and pumps

Disused quarry

Tailrace tunnels

Lower reservoir

TIDAL POWER

The amount of energy available in the world's oceans is enormous. The difficulty is in harnessing it, although there are a number of ways in which this can be done. But the only way that energy is obtained from the oceans at the moment is from tidal power. Like windmills, simple tidal water mills have been in use for a long time and are a very old form of technology. The ebb and flow of tides around the world could be a major source of power in the future. Tidal movements result from the gravitational pull of the Moon and Sun on ocean waters. But only where the difference between the levels of high and low tide is big, is it worthwhile harnessing this power. At present, only the Soviet Union and France have tidal power stations.

TIDAL BARRAGES

The best way to harness tidal power is in the mouth of a large river estuary. A barrage or barrier is constructed between the opposite shores. Tides cause water to flow in and out of the estuary and this movement is used to drive turbines. Plans for a tidal barrage across the Severn Estuary in Britain have been discussed for a number of years. The Bay of Fundy, in North America, is another good site for such a barrage as it has the greatest tidal rise and fall in the world.

THE RANCE BARRAGE

The world's first tidal barrage was built in France across the estuary of the River Rance in Brittany. Its design is different from that of most hydroelectric power stations. The turbines, instead of being in a powerhouse, are inside the barrier itself. The turbines are also of a special design. They can rotate in either direction so that they can be turned by water moving in and out of the estuary, to take advantage of ingoing and outgoing tides.

One problem with this method of producing electricity is that the pressure of the water is about ten times less than that in an average hydroelectric power station. Tidal power stations also cause damage to the environment of the estuary where they are built, because estuaries often have a large amount of unique wildlife. However, tidal power could make an important contribution to the world's total energy supplies.

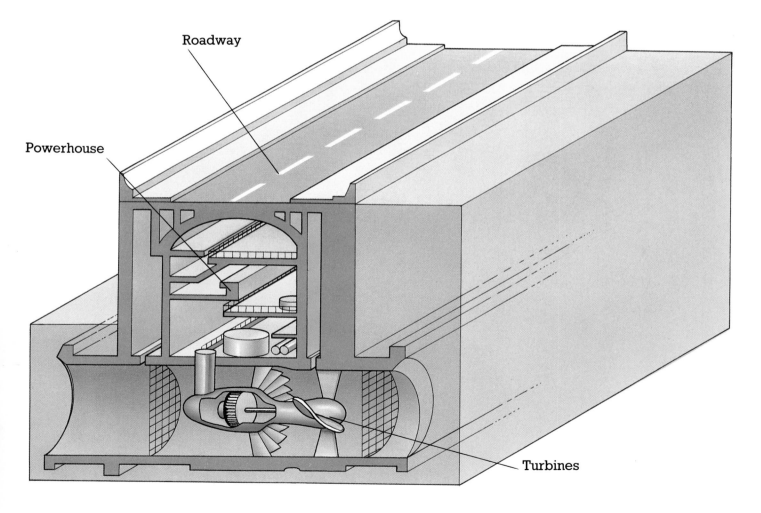

Roadway

Powerhouse

Turbines

SOLAR POWER

Solar power is using energy from the sun to make useful heat or electricity. There are two main ways that this can be done. Heat from the sun (in the form of infrared rays) or light (including ultraviolet rays) can both be used. Solar power is being used increasingly. But it is not a good source of power everywhere. The amount of solar energy available at a particular place depends on its distance from the equator and the amount of cloud. The best areas for solar power are tropical deserts like the Sahara, where there is little cloud and maximum intensity of the Sun's rays. At present, solar energy is most widely used to heat domestic water, although solar cells are used in spacecraft to convert sunlight directly into electricity.

GREENHOUSE

The glass roof and walls of a greenhouse let in the Sun's infrared rays, which are absorbed by plants and the soil. Some of the heat is reemitted as rays that cannot pass back through the glass. So the inside of the greenhouse is kept warm.

Ultraviolet rays   Sun

Infrared rays

HEAT

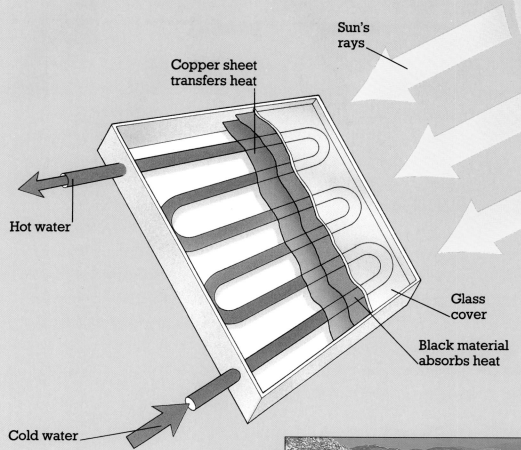

Sun's rays

Copper sheet transfers heat

Hot water

Cold water

Glass cover

Black material absorbs heat

SOLAR PANELS

Water for use in homes can be heated by trapping the Sun's heat between transparent panels of glass and black (heat-absorbent) material. In one design, the heat that is absorbed is transferred to water pipes by a sheet of copper (copper is a good conductor of heat). Cold water is passed through the pipes to be heated as it circulates. The hot water is then piped through a water tank to heat its contents. Millions of these "flat plate" collectors are now in use in countries such as Australia, Israel, and Japan, which receive a great deal of sunlight. The collectors can be placed on the roof of a house and angled toward

the Sun. They can even be used in countries such as Britain, where there is far more cloud, because the periods of sunshine are still long enough to heat water supplies. In 1974, the United States government set aside funds for the design and erection of solar heated buildings.

SOLAR POWER

MAKING ELECTRICITY

The solar energy that falls on the Earth in two weeks is equivalent to all the world's original supplies of coal, oil, and gas. If a small fraction of this could be turned into electricity, we would begin to meet some of our long-term energy needs. An experiment in Albuquerque, New Mexico, has shown one way that the Sun's rays can be converted into electricity. Rows of hundreds of mirrors reflect onto a single collector at the top of a tower, 197 feet high. Water circulates through the collector and is turned into high pressure steam. The steam could be used to drive generators and produce electricity. However, the rows of mirrors have to be turned to follow the Sun, and at present, the scheme is uneconomic. Other similar schemes, known as solar furnaces, have also failed to be economically successful.

Another way to make electricity is to use solar cells (also known as photovoltaic cells). Solar cells make electricity directly from sunlight. But most convert only about 10 percent of the energy that reaches them, and they are expensive to make.

◁ 1000 watt solar cell (inset)
▽ Solar furnace in the Pyrenees, France

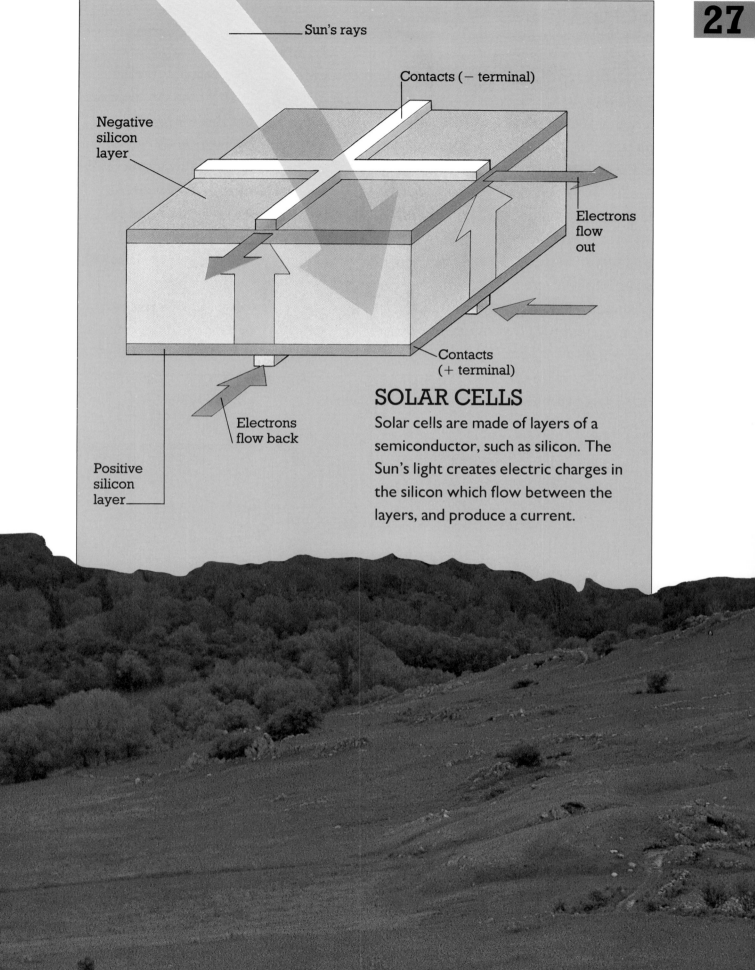

Sun's rays

Contacts (− terminal)

Negative
silicon
layer

Electrons
flow
out

Contacts
(+ terminal)

Electrons
flow back

Positive
silicon
layer

SOLAR CELLS

Solar cells are made of layers of a semiconductor, such as silicon. The Sun's light creates electric charges in the silicon which flow between the layers, and produce a current.

SOLAR POWER

USES OF SOLAR CELLS

Solar cells do not convert a large amount of the energy that reaches them into electricity, and they are very expensive. So they are not economic to use for many purposes. For example, it is unlikely that there will ever be power stations that produce electricity using solar cells. The most common use for solar cells is where only very small amounts of electricity are needed. For example, in solar powered calculators and watches only small cells are needed – which are quite cheap – and it does not matter that the cells are not very efficient. The other main use of solar cells is in satellites. Because satellites are out in space where there is no atmosphere, the sunlight they receive is very strong – there is no atmosphere to filter the light. It is also impossible for satellites to refuel, and if they had to carry all their fuel with them, they would be very heavy to launch. The cost of solar cells is quite small compared to the rest of the cost of a satellite. If solar cells become much more efficient and much cheaper, it is possible that one day they will be used to provide light and even heat for people's homes.

SOLAR POWERED TRANSPORTATION

Solar energy can be used to power transportation. Solar cells are used to make electricity, which drives the vehicle. Many different solar powered cars have been made. But they all have the problem that solar cells are not efficient. The car has to be very small and light, and can usually only carry one person. Solar cars travel slowly, but can cover long distances. They will only work well in places with a great deal of strong sunlight. If a cloud goes across the sun, the car will stop! People have also made solar powered airplanes. These have even more problems than solar powered cars because they need extra energy to get off the ground.

WORLD CLIMATES

Wind, water and solar power depend very much on the world's climate. Wind power depends on the strength of the wind. Water power depends on rain to fill reservoirs behind dams, or on the movement of tides and ocean currents. Solar power depends on the amount of sunlight that is available. It is important to understand the world's climate if we are to use these sources of power effectively. It is difficult to know exactly what the weather will be in a particular place. But we can usually know what the average climate is.

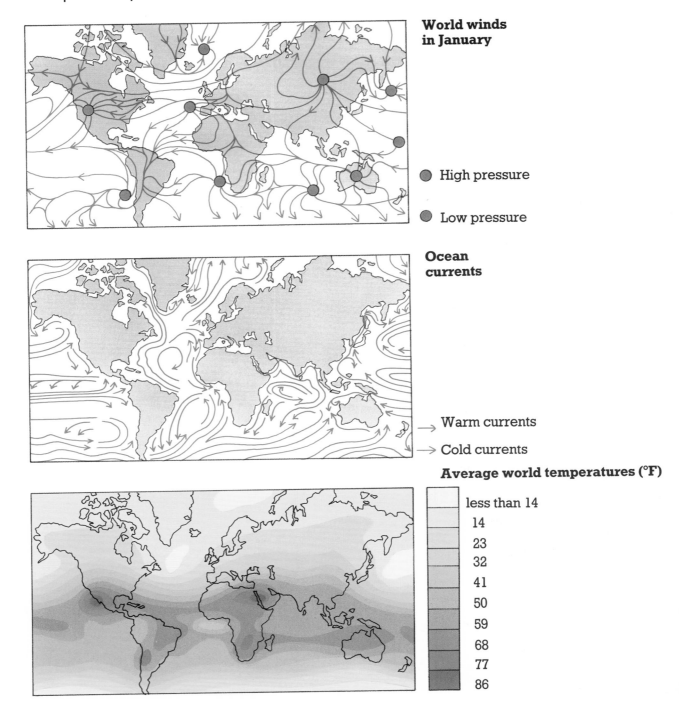

World winds in January

● High pressure

● Low pressure

Ocean currents

→ Warm currents

→ Cold currents

Average world temperatures (°F)

less than 14
14
23
32
41
50
59
68
77
86

GLOSSARY

climate conditions on earth such as amount of sunlight, temperature and rainfall. Climate is another word for the weather.

environment all the things that surround and affect life on earth, including people. This involves the climate and the effects of living things on each other.

fossil fuel fuel that is extracted from the earth and is made from the remains of plants and animals. Coal, oil and gas are fossil fuels.

generator machine that can turn mechanical energy into electricity. In a power station the mechanical energy usually comes from a turbine.

hydroelectricity electricity that is made using water power.

infrared ray form in which heat energy travels across empty space. Heat from the Sun arrives on earth as infrared rays.

renewable energy energy that is produced in a way that does not use something that cannot be replaced (such as coal).

thermal power station power station that produces energy by burning something, such as a fossil fuel.

turbine machine that is driven by the movement of water or a hot gas (such as steam).

wind turbine name that is sometimes used for a windmill.

USEFUL ADDRESSES

Conservation and Environmental Protection Division
Agricultural Stablization and Conservation Service
Department of Agriculture
14th Street & Independence Avenue SW
Washington, D.C. 20250

Answers inquiries.

Global Water
1629 K Street NW
Suite 500
Washington, D.C. 20006

Provides inquiry and referral services.

Greenpeace
1161 Connecticut Avenue NW
Washington, D.C. 20009

Pollution Probe Foundation
12 Madison Avenue
Toronto, Ontario M5R 2S1

Answers inquiries, provides information and referral services, distributes publications.

Water Resources Research Institute
202 Hargis Hall
Auburn, AL. 3649

Answers general inquiries.

INDEX